HOW IS YOUR PRAYER LIFE?

HOW IS YOUR PRAYER LIFE?

ROSELINE UDOETUK

Eleviv Publishing Group info@elevivpublishing.com elevivpublishing.com

CONTENTS

Dedication   viii

APPRECIATION

PREFACE

INTRODUCTION

1	THE CALL TO PRAY	12
2	EVERYBODY NEEDS PRAYERS	20
3	PRAYER IS A MUST	24
4	YOUR PRAYER IS YOUR WEAPON	27
5	THE FUTURE OF TOMORROW LIES WITH GOD	30
6	PRAYER IS THE KEY	32
7	AUTHORITY OF BLESSINGS	35
8	WHY PRAY?	40

9	PRAYER: CHANGE AGENT	44
10	WHAT PRAYER DOES	47
11	PRAYER CHANGES CIRCUMSTANCES	51
12	PRAY WITH FAITH	53
13	PRAY WITH HUMILITY	57
14	PRAY TO RECEIVE NOT TO GRUMBLE	60
15	PRAYER CHANGES DESTINIES	63
16	PRAYER TURNS LIFE BATTLES INTO BLESSINGS	69
17	PRAYER BRINGS YOUR EXPECTATION INTO REALITY	74

EPILOGUE

ABOUT THE AUTHOR

REFLECTIONS	81
DAILY TO-DO LIST	85
PRAYER POINTS	87
PRAYER POINTS	89

Copyright © 2021 by Roseline Udoetuk

All rights reserved. Published in the United States by Eleviv Publishing Group. No part of this book may be reproduced, stored in a retrieval system, or transmitted in any form or by any means, electronic, mechanical, photocopying, recording, or otherwise, without the prior written permission of the author, except as provided by U.S.A. copyright law or in the case of brief quotations embodied in critical articles and reviews.

The publisher does not have any control over and does not assume any responsibility for the author or third-party websites or their content.

Holy Bible, New Living Translation, copyright © 1996, 2004, 2007, 2013, 2015 by Tyndale House Foundation. Used by permission of Tyndale House Publishers Inc., Carol Stream, Illinois 60188.

All rights reserved. New Living, NLT, and the New Living Translation logo are registered trademarks of Tyndale House Publishers.

ISBN: 978-1-952744-36-5
eISBN: 978-1-952744-37-2

Cover Design: Charles Fate (Notch Design)
Published By:
Eleviv Publishing Group
Centerville, OH 45458
elevivpublishing.com
info@elevivpublishing.com
1-281-857-0569
1-800-353-0635

First Printing, 2021

Published and Printed in the United States of America

10 9 8 7 6 5 4 3 2 1

DEDICATION

Without God, nothing is possible. Therefore, I thank God Almighty for His Words and inspiration for me to write this book. When the Holy Spirit inspired me to write this book, I was ready. After a while, I felt I did not have enough information to allow me to start writing. But with persistent prayer and expecting God's voice to speak to me, I was able to start and finish writing this book. I could not have done it if it wasn't for His call and purpose for me.

PRAYER IS THE WEAPON TO OVERCOME LIFE BATTLES AND WITHOUT PRAYERS, THERE ARE NO MIRACLES.

APPRECIATION

I give God the praise and adoration for His faithfulness over me. When I was writing this book, I didn't believe I would finish it, but God's grace granted me wisdom, patience, and understanding. I want to appreciate my family for their love and support. Without them seeing the vision of God in me, completing this book would have been the most challenging path for me.

PREFACE

The world was meant to be perfect until Satan came and deceived Man to fall. The fall for everyone happened the day Eve tasted the fruit from the Tree of Knowledge. The Bible reminds us that all have fallen and have come short of the glory of God. In other words, we have all wronged God in one way or another, and the curse of disobedience from one man and woman is upon every man. However, God is a God of second chances. He is ready to make us rise again through our dedication to Him, serving His purpose through prayer, reading, and doing His Word.

A fall is for every man, but the rise is an individual decision. It is your choice to rise. Remember that your rising is for God's glory and praise because His purpose for you is to rise above and beyond all imagination. As you read this book, I pray that you will find Christ in your heart and accept Him as the beginning and the end of all things.

Satan is in constant battle with our lives because he wants to destroy God's purpose for our lives. The race of life is more than just getting up from sleep and getting ready to accomplish your daily tasks. The race of this present time is to overcome the totality of turmoil, failure, war, sorrow, disappointment, anguish, and barriers into the breakthrough of God's inherent grace and favor to achieve His clear and designed purpose for the reason of our existence.

The only weapon to fight the battles of life is prayer. So long as you are in this world, you are on a battlefield and a race to save your soul;

the world is filled with daily wars, some seen and others unseen. Unpredictably, you are constantly defending yourself at work with your CEO, manager, or supervisor, over being accused of what you did not do or should have done. Then, you begin to wonder how that happened. All of these are happening because Satan is at work to ruin you and jeopardize all you have spent years building.

Sometimes, you get confused about what to do, seeing how many wars fell on you in different places, and you seem to have asked yourself, "what did I do to go through all these troubles?" The answer is that you didn't do anything wrong. It's simply because the devil is competing with God over your life and happiness. The devil will do anything to win you for himself if you give up on the truth of God's Word, which is reading your Bible, prayer, fasting, meditation, and supplication.

The devil will then be glad to throw a party with his agents that he has succeeded and won you over to himself. However, suppose you fight him with the Spirit of God through fervent prayers and fasting, meditation, and supplication. In that case, he will flee to a weaker person, available to him, and then regret ever coming your way. Read *1Peter 5:8 (NIV), "Be alert and of sober mind. Your enemy the devil prowls around like a roaring lion looking for someone to devour."*

The devil is constantly at work to fight. For you to overcome him, you must fight him with the only weapon he dislikes, and that is prayer. Satan is not a professional businessman, who comes to your house in a suit and a tie, knocks on your door for you to open the door so that he convinces you to buy his merchandise. Satan is a perpetrator who will do anything to throw worries and confusion at you to make you give up on yourself and God. Why? He is unhappy that God loves you. So, he plans to throw fear at you. A fight against Satan is not a physical fight; it's a fight with the Holy Spirits' help to defeat his satanic agenda. You were created to win, and for you to win, you must fight to overcome. Overcoming the fight of the unseen is not with canal mind, but with divine intervention. If you must fight, then you must develop a habit of standing and resisting the scheme of Satan through prayers and fasting.

Prayer is a habit that must be learned and practiced daily. To pray is the willingness to submit to the will of God. Most people pray, and later, they relent. At the same time, some people anticipate praying but never make the time to pray. Some want to pray, but something always gets in their way, for example, work, children, tiredness, stress, and forgetfulness. Some cannot pray because the location or the environment is not conducive for them. In contrast, some do not know what to pray for or about or how to pray. Some say, "Well, it doesn't matter. It's what it is. What will happen, will happen, no matter what."

The beauty of praying to God is that God is everywhere. He is in your bathroom, office, work, school, even in the desert and ocean. He is truly everywhere! God does not hear our prayers based on how long we pray, what days we pray, or where we are. But He hears and answers us based on the sincerity of our hearts to Him. Prayer requires adequate responsibility, commitment, accountability, and time. Being responsible for your prayer is very important. You don't pray because you want to pray; you pray because it's a must. No employer will hire you because they want to. They must employ you because they need you. Prayer is a spiritual need, and for your needs to be met, prayer must be adequately supplied each day.

Jesus did not have a need to pray because He is the Son of God, but because Jesus came in human flesh and demonstrated to us that prayer is mandatory. While Jesus was in the flesh, He suffered, lamented, cried, and wished this cup of His death could be taken away from Him. Prayer is a need, not a want. It is easy not to wear a particular outfit because it's too tight or too short. It's easy to choose a different outfit that fits your body properly, but we don't have a choice with our challenges. They come when we don't want or expect them. The only way to overcome our challenges is through prayer. When you deprive yourself of food, you inhibit your growth and nourishment. But when you deprive yourself of prayers, you give way for Satan to rise above, to destroy and kill you.

Prayer is the spiritual food that nurtures the soul, body, spirit, and mind. Jesus could have asked His Father in heaven to send Legions of

Angels to fight His battle, or perhaps, He could have been commuting from heaven to earth daily. After all, He has the power to do anything that He wants to do. But the purpose of His coming was to suffer for us and die on the cross at the appointed time. So, He decided to come as a human being to feel pain, cry, and walk barefoot with other people and even had no place He called His home. The purpose of Christ coming to the world was to alleviate our suffering, pain and make our burdens lighter.

Prayer is necessary for your daily life. If you must win the battles of this life, you must pray to conquer. It is time to move out of your comfort zone and walk into your part of freedom. We sometimes want to settle where we are because it's convenient and easy for us to go and come back without any hassle. But sometimes, the easy part of life is the reason for our trouble.

Let the truth be told; there is time for everything, and nothing goes for nothing. The difference in life begins with the step you take today. Instead of sitting down to be consoled, take a step into prayer to gain access to your breakthrough. Life is sweet, but the stages of life can be rough, challenging, and even discouraging. But when you put God first, everything will work in your favor. One of the tools that Satan uses to weaken us daily is to stop us from praying. Prayer is a powerful tool of breakthrough. It doesn't matter how terrible your situation may be or how awful your story may sound. The way to make a difference is through prayer.

INTRODUCTION

Prayer moves mountains. Jesus said if you have faith like the mustard seed, you will say to the mountain to move from here to there, and it will move. Obedience brings you honor, and prayer brings you victory. God uses our prayers to refine us. God is the fire, and you are the flame. According to Zechariah 2:5 (NIV), *"And I myself will be a wall of fire around it,' declares the Lord, 'and I will be its glory within."* The flame cannot bring fire without you blowing the smoke. You must light a candle for it to burn. You cannot fight a war without a weapon, and a weapon cannot perform its function without you getting it ready to be used.

Life is a battle. The only way to win the battles of life is with prayer. We often work hard to achieve success, and later in life, we seem to be completely starting over. Most of the time, some people graduate from college, own homes of their dreams, get married, have children, and at the peak of the time to enjoy their lifelong hard work, they find themselves dwindling with challenges, fear, death of loved ones, sickness, and diseases. Some end up losing all that they have worked for. The fear of starting all over sets in and eventually leads to depression. Some end up dying from cardiac arrest caused by stress.

There is an invisible power that comes with prayer, and the potential of your prayer is to act upon the will of God and for you to give thanks for the unforeseen that is yet to manifest to reality. The importance of prayer cannot be over-emphasized. The world is full of uncertainties. In this time of uncertainty, the only thing that can avail for us is prayer. Prayer is not just communication but an avenue that draws us nearer to God. Most people see prayer or praying as a waste of time because they pray for a short time and want to receive an answer in a short time.

Most people assume that you only pray when things fall out of place. Prayer is not gambling, where you put in a bet to play and then wait for the result to be announced in a day or two. Prayer is an act to trust in and wait on God. Prayer is your entitlement. It is your right and privilege to pray, and the more you pray, the more you see yourself better and feel better. The most important part of prayer or praying is the closeness between God and us. Prayer brings your intimacy with God. We cannot fall in love with someone without seeing that person and understanding him or her. Prayer justifies our intimacy with God. So, the more we pray, the closer we get or feel close to God, and the more we see Him.

God is a Spirit, and those who worship Him must worship Him in spirit and truth; John 4:24. The only way we can embrace the spirit of the divine power of God is through prayer. It loosens our spiritual bondage. Each of us was born with a purpose. But sometimes, the purpose that we were born into can be challenged, and without prayer, we cannot reach the destination of that purpose for our lives.

Before God created us, He knew what we would become. He predestined our future based on His designed plans and purpose for us. Remember that the devil is always at work, day and night, to counteract God's plans and purpose for our lives. If we don't steer our minds in prayer, we cannot overcome his force of opposition.

Sometimes, we start out well in our plans, and just when it's time to reap the benefits of our efforts, we fall, and the struggle to rise again becomes frustrating. That's because we took God out of our plans. I will agree with you if you say that because you didn't plan out well, that's why the plan did not come out well. But how can we plan well if God is not involved? God is the master planner…our master planner. If we do not involve Him in our plans, they will not work, and it may seem like a fruit coming out of the tree. But sooner or later, the sun will kill the roots of our efforts, and the tree will die instantly.

| 1 |

THE CALL TO PRAY

One of the positive things that I have experienced in my relationship with God is His Love throughout my life. The emphasis of God's Love for us is referenced in **1 John 4-9**, *"Beloved, let us love one another: for love is of God, and everyone that loveth is born of God and knoweth God. He that loveth not knoweth not God; for God is love." In this, was manifested the love of God toward us because God sent his only begotten Son into the world, that we might live through him.* Experiencing God's love has given me the insight to know that no matter how tall the mountain may be, His love is faithful and beyond comprehension, regardless of circumstances.

Experiencing God's love begins with making a connection with God. Making a connection with God begins with your acceptance that Jesus Christ is a Son of God and was raised from the dead. Without a spiritual connection with God, there is no relationship with Him. Your relationship with God is not just a mere relationship but an absolute relationship that brings favor, peace, promotion, victory, and testimonies.

Anyone who receives favor from his employer has had some connection with their employer. Whether in the military, church work, or secular services, anyone who is promoted has built a long-lasting relationship with their job experiences to the extent that they no longer worry about what to expect because of the long-lasting connection with the job assignment.

Knowing God is different from experiencing God because one can know God's name but do not have a relationship with God to experience His benevolences. Experiencing God requires your energy and your senses. It takes energy to work and insights to understand our environment. In other words, to experience God, you must allow God's power to flow inside you, and you must allow God's movement to control your senses.

Experiencing God is a lifelong journey, which involves completely surrendering all your plans and purposes to Him and trusting Him in all endeavors. God is love, and his love reaches out to everyone on earth, but not everyone who has tasted His love can testify of the goodness of Him because they lack that sense of God's connection to know that the sun and rain are the gifts of God's love.

There are a few steps that one must follow to experience God:

Submit: The **first** step to experience God's presence is to submit to His will. Submission is the hardest part of experiencing God but is the most realm of blessing. You must take the place of a servant and let God be the master of all decisions. *"Submit yourselves, therefore to God. Resist the devil, and he will flee from you." James 4:7* Submission is the first part of knowing God, and without submission, nothing can be accomplished.

Read: Reading the Word of God gives us the understanding to know God and to yield to His commands; reading the bible will connect you directly to God because the Bible is God's spoken prophesy. 2 Timothy 3:16 *"All scripture is given by inspiration of God, and is profitable for doctrine, for reproof, for correction, and for instruction in righteousness":*

Pray: Praying to God is an act of communicating to Him and waiting expectantly on His voice. *"And it shall come to pass, that before they call, I will answer; and while they are yet speaking, I will hear." Isaiah 65:24*

Write: Writing down Bible verses and God's Words will help you connect strongly with God.

Meditate: Meditating on the Word of God and remembering Bible passages will help you know that God's mercies are new every day

Praise: Singing and praising God in all circumstances will release strength from heaven upon you. *"Therefore, shall ye lay up these my words in your heart and your soul, and bind them for a sign upon your hand, that they may be as frontlets between your eyes." Deuteronomy 11:18*

Worship: The atmosphere of worship and glorifying God will release God's power over you. *"He that hath clean hands, and a pure heart; who hath not lifted up his soul unto vanity, nor sworn deceitfully. He shall receive the blessing from the LORD, and righteousness from the God of his salvation." Psalm 24:4*

Give: No matter the circumstances, give thanks to God for all things comes from Him, and His hands are never tied to hold you through any situation. *"Give unto the LORD the glory due to His name; Worship the LORD in the beauty of holiness." Psalm 29:2*

After reading those steps, experiencing the uncommon blessings of God and His mercies are as simple as ASAP. Something must take effect in your heart today. Your heart must be released to God's anointing, and your mouth must be open to make a declaration of your freedom and breakthrough.

Follow the ASAP Steps Below to Unravel Your Freedom in Christ Jesus.

The acronym of ASAP is:
A-Accept Jesus as your Lord and personal Savior.
S-Submit to God's will and purpose.
A-Appreciate God's plans for you.
P-Pray daily to be covered under God's umbrella.

Without acceptance, there is no repentance (and without repentance), there is no access to God's goodwill and freedom. Without submission to the will of God, there is no hope and trust during trials. Without appreciating the plans of God in your life, there is no open door to joy. Without prayer, your spiritual privileges to overcome will be declined.

Life comes with so many unexpected circumstances. Therefore, the reality is that life happens. But how can we be sure that we can control the unexpected? When we learn to align ourselves with God, we will understand that man has only one way of solving one problem, but God has many ways of solving that same problem.

Often, I hear people say, let's face reality; it's what it is. No doubt about the unexpected being a reality, of a truth, good and bad things happen to everybody, God's plan does not mean that people who repent will not cry or go through tribulations. After all Christ said in Matthew 10:22, *"And ye shall be hated of all men for my name's sake: but he that endureth to the end shall be saved."* Endurance and perseverance are the ladders that will carry you to lasting joy. But the question is, how can we find joy when it seems like life is failing us?

A friend once asked me, "why do people boast that the Lord is good when life experience is sadness and failure?" I told him that sadness and failure are of this world, but the joy and overcoming are of God. "I have never been happy for once; all I've experienced is rejection and agony," my friend concluded.

Happiness and joy are two different things. When we buy a car, we experience happiness because we can buy what we want. When the car develops problems and needs repair, we experience sadness and wish we didn't have to buy that car. Joy is a profound indwelling excitement that fills your heart, no matter the circumstances. It is okay to get angry when a situation doesn't turn out the way it was anticipated. However, one can be assured that God is in control when all hope fails.

Here's the truth, everyone in this world has a coin of their problem, and the problem is part of God's purpose for our lives, but when we don't understand that the solution to our problems lies in God's hands, we aimlessly fight our problems alone and end up giving up. Rather than giving up on your situation, close your eyes and take a moment to ponder on who you are, why you were created, and why you are facing these challenges. If you can find answers to those questions, then you'd have realized that there is a greater power in you, asking you to call on Him because He will answer you.

Nehemiah was a noble character in the Bible. He was not a famous prophet, but he portrayed a noble character of what it means to cry to God for mercy. Nehemiah 1:1-10: Nehemiah heard that the sin of his fathers and the nation has caused the wall of Jerusalem to crumble; he cried and fasted to God and pleaded for mercies to rebuild the walls of Jerusalem. He asked God to grant him access by King Artaxerxes to rebuild the walls of his father, the next day when Nehemiah approached the king, and the king was surprised to see Nehemiah's countenance. So, the king asked Nehemiah what his problem was, and he told him and requested that he should grant him the resources to build his father's wall.

God does not forsake anyone but only keeps quiet at those who do not want Him. But when the desire to seek God comes, His desire to perform His miracle will also come.

Today is your day of breakthrough because God is about to turn things around in your life. Always remember that life is a beautiful gift that comes in different colors and shades of experiences with joy, pain, blessing, tears, happiness, peace, loss, gain, disappointments, and surprises. However, there is a massive difference for those who trust in the Lord, knowing that no matter what life brings, there is the assurance of peace, hope, and joy.

The Power of Prayer

Without prayer, there is no miracle. Therefore, the need for prayer is now. This book is meant to help guide you to experience God's supernatural ways and His faithfulness in a brand-new way. Without prayer, there is no freedom, and without devotion, there is no peace, and without praise, there is no completion. There is no one way for success, but there is only one way for peace. The only way to find peace and tranquility in the storm is through Jesus.

Jesus said in John 14:27, "Peace I leave with you, my peace I give to you; not as the world gives do I give to you. Let not your heart be troubled, neither let it be afraid." Have you noticed that the world is getting more successful with technology innovation, increased market revenue, high turnover profit, higher education, status, and increased knowledge? Yet, the world lacks peace! Why is it so? Well, because many people seek after the lust of this world to gratify their immediate needs for the flesh and then neglect the glory of God that comes with joy.

In this book, I hope that you are going to develop a mindset of prayer. Jeremiah 33:3 says, *"Call to me, and I will answer you, and show you great and mighty things, which you do not know."* God has good in stock for those that call on Him. God is not a partial God that many people make it sound. He is a good God of outstanding rewards, who rewards according to your heart's desire. A farmer who wants to harvest plenty must make more room to plant plenty.

I will take you through a series of prayer topics to build your confidence in praying to God and a gradual process to develop a strong relationship with God. Each chapter in this book will give you a spirit-filled prayer life that will connect you and get you closer to God. As you read this book, please read to develop an intimate relationship with God and closeness to His supernatural breakthrough. Prayer is an exercise of faith and waiting patiently on the things that are not yet seen.

Before you embark on the next page, please take time to answer the following questions:
Are you ready to repent?
Are you ready to pray?
Are you ready to wait?
Are you ready to receive?

If your answer is yes, pray this simple prayer:

Lord Jesus, I am a sinner. Today, I am blessed to know that your blood on the cross of Calvary has washed me clean. Today, I present myself afresh to you, and I humble myself in your presence because you are my God, and there is none like you. I am saved by grace from today onwards, and I am made whole from my past and present sins.

Lord, I thank you for the opportunity to develop a relationship with you. Please grant me the spirit to depend on you, and give me the understanding of your Word, and help me to stand justified and victorious on the solid rock of Jesus when everything thing
   else fails.

Lord, today, I surrender my weakness to you. Please, may you uproot from me any bad seed, and may your good seed of love, joy, and gladness be planted and germinate in me to the glory of your name. Lord, I give myself to you as a living sacrifice, worthy to serve and worship you in spirit and Holiness. Amen. May God bless you for taking a bold step into the Kingdom of God. Congratulations!

The next step is for you to develop a strong tie with God. If you do not have a home church, go online, look for Christ denomination church, and start attending. Be sure to let the pastor or the church minister know what areas of services you would like to uptake as your services to God.

Prayer: *Father, as I begin my journey in writing this book, may you open my eyes to see you, and may your peace and joy fill my heart. Help me know that you are my strength and peace and that no matter what may come my way, I will still know that you are here for me. Amen!*

| 2 |

EVERYBODY NEEDS PRAYERS

Riches do not solve spiritual needs. They only solve material problems. Jesus said in Matthew 4:4, *"Man shall not live by bread alone, but by every word that proceedeth out of the mouth of God."* We eat food to nourish the flesh, but prayer nourishes the spirit and soul.

Prayer will bring you closer to God, and your burden of pains will be lighter. Without prayer, there is no solution. This may sound outdated, but the truth is that even people who thought they could do it without prayer are now going from church to church, parish to parish, and from one prayer house to another, calling one prophet after another, seeking aimless blessings, answers, and miracles.

While there is nothing wrong with finding people to pray for you, the most efficacious prayer is knowing why you are praying and who you are praying to. Most people only seek prayer when things are unbearable for them, when they remember God, or when their last resort failed them.

God is not the last choice, but the first and only. When people seek God as their last resort, they feel that God is taking too long to answer their prayers, and later, they feel discouraged and think that there is no God. Without communication, there is no relationship. Proverb 8:17 says, *"I love them that love me, and those that seek me early shall find me."* The more you communicate with God, the closer your relationship with Him, and the quicker His response to your prayer is.

Effective prayer is not how long we pray; it's how closer we are to God. Jumpstart your prayer life today to live beyond all falls. I said falls because there is a fall in everyone's life, but the grace to rise is from God. Proverb 24:16, *"For a just man falleth seven times, and riseth up again: but the wicked shall fall into mischief."*

Indeed, everyone has fallen, but the grace of God has found all. Believe me, not all that has fallen will rise unless one uses the ticket of grace to unlock the freedom. Jesus Christ, the only Son of God, born of human flesh, came to sacrifice His life for the grace of all to merit the freedom of God's kingdom. Nobody did anything to receive the grace, not by works or might, but through His blood, we are chosen by grace to a new path of life through the savior. However, there is still work to do. The work of grace is to denounce the ungodly and forsake our old ways of life and live anew in Christ Jesus.

We are children of God, but did you know that it takes sacrifice and work for a father to love His child? God wants us always to pray; the more we pray, the more we build our trust and hope in God. It takes the energy of love, respect, obedience, commitment, and trust to develop a strong relationship with father and child. Without this energy, there is no solid relationship. We are often told that no situation is permanent, but sometimes situations can become permanent if we don't seek God's presence. The more we seek God, the stronger our relationship with Him and the more energized we become to overcome.

There is power in prayer, and until we pray, we cannot understand the graceful power of what prayer can do even in the worst situation. Where grace is mentioned, it means there is all-sufficient power bestowed upon to act beyond the ordinary. This book is meant to also enlighten your mind to know that it cannot be proven without God doing it. Our lives are not television shows, where we go to the movie theatre and watch the latest movie or shows, and when it ends, everybody goes home. Life is a continuum process of living, with unplanned path of challenges and discouragement. Without adequate dedication and devotion to God, life will seem like or become a burden of pain and unfulfillment.

Often, we are bombarded with vigorous life challenges. Sometimes, we question how we can navigate through these different difficult paths. But, if I may ask, what is your prayer life, how often do you pray, and what is your relationship with God? Everybody is calling God, but how many people really know God? Calling God is different from knowing Him. When we know God, we put God in front and above everything else.

The Word of God says, *"With God, all things are possible."* There is no guarantee that you will not have problems in your life, but there is a guarantee that your burden will be lighter. Psalm 9: 9 says, *"The LORD also will be a refuge for the oppressed, A refuge in times of trouble."* Are you worried about your life, children, marriage, finances, employment, health, spouse, and freedom? It's not too late to take charge of the things you cannot change; neither is it too late for God to change what we thought could not be changed. There is no perfect time to let God change your situation than now. I pray that today is your day of victory. May God accelerate into your life to change the hopelessness and what seems like unchangeable conditions in your life. Amen

Most times, we hear professionals say, *"We got this,"* and suddenly, what they got becomes "we tried our best." We cannot blame them because they are humans like us, and they did not know that the situation could unexpectedly be disappointing. We also know that they are not God, but humans, just as you and I. The only difference is the title attached to their names.

When your problem keeps you awake at night or makes your thought go places without coming back with a solid solution, it's time to realize that it can't be solved without God's intervention.

Prayer: *Holy Spirit, you are all-sufficient and all-wise God. There is nothing you cannot do. All powers belong to you. Lord, please, may your power rest upon me today to experience you supernaturally. Amen.*

| 3 |

PRAYER IS A MUST

We don't want to pray or feel like praying most of the time, but we expect miracles to happen. When we don't find the expected miracle or answer, we go from one church to another, looking for a quick and microwavable miracle.

Most people have stumbled into a satanic church, all in the name of searching for a miracle. In the process, the devil uses these people as his agents, giving them the material things they yearn for, yet they cannot find that joy or inner peace.

Prayer is or should be our spiritual food and the weapon to fight all battles. Without prayers or having faith, there is no miracle. Jesus said, *"pray without ceasing."* The hour of pray without ceasing has come. Our Lord Jesus foresaw today, and He warned us to pray and not slumber. Nobody can say they do not need to pray because we all have problems in our lives.

Therefore, we cannot say that we don't have any problem. For as long as you are alive and have a soul, prayer is your companion because it is a sacred ritual to God. When you pray vehemently with a clean heart, the God of clean hands will release His powers and protection over you.

Prayer Gives Peace

Show me a prayerful person, and I will tell you how peaceful the person is. Prayer brings peace and tranquility. When life challenges are rough, prayer gives us peace of mind to know that God is inside our situations. No situation is above God, and no circumstances can overcome God's plan. Remember that God lives in heaven, and the earth is His footstool. Therefore, all situations are under His feet.

Why Do We Face Challenges?

We face challenges because of the fall of sin from one man and one woman; our first parents in the Garden of Eden ate the fruit from the forbidden tree that God commanded them not to eat. Life challenges came into existence when they, Adam and Eve, crossed the boundary of *"thou shall not eat the tree of knowledge."*

Everyone born of a woman will face one life's battle or another. But there is only one way to overcome life challenges. Sometimes, it seems like life is too hard on us, and we feel like giving up. The truth is that the promise of God in Isaiah 41:18 says, *"I will open rivers in high places, and fountains amid the valleys: I will make the wilderness a pool of water, and the dry land springs of water."* It's for you to claim.

I don't care what challenges may have come your way, or how sorrowful your life has been, or who has abandoned or neglected you for one reason or the other; God is about to turn your tears into joy. But you must trust God for miracles to happen in your life. God does not perform magic. He performs miracles! The miracles of God manifest all year round.

The only way to overcome life battles is through prayer. Prayer is the master key that unlocks your victory. If Jesus could pray before the beginning of His ministry, then we are all bound to pray, lest the problem of this world will be too overwhelming for us.

| 4 |

YOUR PRAYER IS YOUR WEAPON

A life without prayer is like a flower garden without water and sunlight. I grew up in a spiritual home, and my father made it mandatory for us to pray. At some point, I thought that we were compelled to pray outside our will, but unbeknownst to me that my father wanted us to know that the only weapon to overcome the unforeseen fights and battles is through prayer.

David said to Goliath, *"you have come with weapon and spear, but I have come in the name of the Lord."* If David did not pray, Goliath would have given his flesh to the birds of the earth. But through prayer and his trust in God, the 6 feet tall Goliath fell dead on the ground with just a stone throw at him. If you don't teach a child the difference between hot water and cold water, the child will think that all waters are the same. There is power, and there are powers. *"The name of the Lord is a strong tower. The righteous run into it and be safe."* Proverb 18:10

The incredible power of God is indispensable. It is capable of breaking the cedar and loosening any chain. Prayer brings liberty and victory. The more we become acquainted with prayer, the more spiritually we grow, and the closer we are to God, the more we unveil our victory and divine intervention. Prayer is not meant to be perfect but to draw us closer to God, build a solid foundation of our relationship with God, and reveal His purpose for us.

Ever asked what God's purpose for you is? The purpose of God for you is to rise above everything. No matter the depth of your situation or sorrow, the purpose of God supersedes all forces. When Queen Esther was faced with the pressure of Haman to destroy the Jews, Esther did what any woman in power could not do. When I say a woman in power, I mean a woman who was practically married to the king had nothing to worry about.

Still, wisdom taught her that when there are forces of power playing pranks of authority, the highest authority is God, who can turn things around without seeking officials to vote for His plans. Esther deprived herself of food and wine and denounced herself the kingdom power, to seek the supernatural power that is stronger than all powers through prayer and fasting. After her three days of fasting, the story of Haman became different. Haman was not only dethroned but he was also stripped of his position and power before he was finally destroyed.

When God is at work, no one can stand to fight. When all hope is lost, there is only one hope left. God is your last hope and the only chance to defeat your fight. Stop procrastinating about praying to God over your problems. Start today to pray. No situation can outweigh the powers of God. Not even your problems. That problem, condition, or turbulence in your life has a solution. Where or when men fail is the beginning of God's mighty power.

When Nehemiah began rebuilding the city of Jerusalem, many people laughed at him, told him that his hands would soon be tired and would no longer build the city. He prayed to God, asking Him to strengthen his hands that they may be able to finish building the city. Prayer is not child's play. It's an act to cause an effect of change. When people think that your problem has not turned around, don't let fear or intimidation weigh you down or take your courage. Pray to God earnestly, and indeed, you will see that God's plan for you is beyond description.

Prayer: *O Heavenly Father, the Maker of heaven and earth, the God who was never created but created everything and all living creatures. Today, Lord, may you open my eyes to see your glory, and may every good thing that was dead in me come back to life to the glory of your name. I surrender my life to you to your glory, and may your peace that surpasses all human knowledge rest upon me today and forever. Amen.*

| 5 |

THE FUTURE OF TOMORROW LIES WITH GOD

No one knows what tomorrow holds. Nobody! But with prayer and obedience to God, we can be assured that the walls are secured no matter the severe threat of the future or present.

God is a Father of all possibilities. Without one tasting to see the act of God's love, we cannot understand His capabilities. See where the world is today? We cannot predict what could happen next. Anger and rage of destruction are everywhere. We no longer feel safe. Our children are now questioning wickedness, and we don't even have answers to their questions.

The world is in chaos and disarray. We no longer know what to expect, but we can expect to understand that no one can be against us when God is with us. While we cannot anticipate our tomorrow, we can start today to walk into our future by letting God take over completely. The future is God's fulfillment of His promises, but how do we know if God has promises for our future? The first promise of God for us was in Genesis 1:28: After God formed man and woman in the Garden of Eden, He gave them a promise and said, *"And God blessed them, and God said unto them, Be fruitful, and multiply, and replenish the earth, and subdue it, and have dominion over the fish of the sea, and over the fowl of the air, and over every living thing that moved upon the earth."*

God gave us a command to be in control of everything. But sin got into the world. Therefore, how can we still be sure that the command to be fruitful and multiply is still our right? While the deed committed in the garden of Eden cannot be undone, our God is merciful and compassionate. He does not withhold the sins of His chosen people and will not turn His back on those that call upon Him.

We are told in Jeremiah that God said, *"before I formed you, I knew you, and I chose you."* In other words, your future lies in the hands of God. When God is in control, nothing can fall out of control.

| 6 |

PRAYER IS THE KEY

Our Lord Jesus Christ could not overlook the importance of praying daily. The key to overcoming the unprecedented future is prayer. Life is full of shocks. As much as we study the process of living organisms, their behavior, the classes of living organisms and species in biology class, there is still something that eludes scientific knowledge. Tomorrow is not in our control but God's control. Even today! Meteorologists can predict weather forecasts. However, they cannot predict our lives in the next five years or seconds. Everyone's life is in the hands of our Creator. We do not know what the future holds for us, but indeed, our future lies with God. We cannot predict what will happen in the next minute of our time, but God sees every second, minute, and hour and can undo any circumstances meant to consume us. God has the final say in your life, and no matter the situation and the degree of your circumstances, the power of prayer can make a turning point today in your life.

The doctors can diagnose sickness and predict the expected time of a person's death due to the underlying risk factor of that sickness. Still, God has the final say. When God says yes, no one can say no. Since we have carefully studied human development, we have not learned the cause of human challenges. Scientists are humans, and they also have challenges. If you take a scientist out of the laboratory, they will tell you the numerous unprecedented war and challenges that eludes their expectations.

We can study the clouds to know if it will rain or not, but no one has studied to predict when wars will start or when challenges will crawl into our lives. Predictions of war in this world are not yet in any textbook, and not because no one would like to study how war comes to crumble our lives, but because no one can see tomorrow. Wars are trials that come in different dimensions. They can come through rain, sun, snow, children, family, vehicles, or even the foods we eat. It is hard to predict that a sweet and loving marriage will crumble and lead to divorce or one spouse murdered by the same person who vowed to love and cherish them.

How can we possibly predict that a marriage built on trust and love, with everything looking perfect, will one day turn into a nightmare? Why should we build wealth today and then find ourselves struggling to survive later in life? Why should the economy crumble into recession? How can we predict that the home we bought and signed to become ours will suddenly turn back to the bank for a foreclosure? How could you predict that the lovely man or woman you married will suddenly die and leave you lonely and heartbroken? How can we anticipate that the precious child you gave birth to will one day become your enemy or take your life? How can anyone predict that a father will sexually abuse his daughter and even get her pregnant one day? Can it be possible to predict that the man or woman you solemnly vowed to love will become a monster you see in the movies?

The devil is not in favor of building us, but rather, he wants to destroy us. Sometimes or most times, we are the devils by the choices we make. There is no knowledge, power, and status in any academic attainment or level of higher education that can comprehend the war of this present world except by God's wisdom through prayer and fasting can we overcome the suffering of this world.

Tomorrow lies in God's hands; the unforeseen and the unpredictable aspect of every living creature is in the naked and unhidden eyes of God. We sleep at night and wake up in the morning. Other than knowing the date of each day and time for that moment, we don't know anything about what could happen the next minute because no one knows what each day carries or will bring. But God has assigned His purpose and blessings for each day of every week and season. However, somedays we wake up, we wish that the challenges we face do not exist or should not be.

God did not create us to throw us into a terrible world, but Man's sinful nature has made the world terrible. For this purpose, we choose to make it right, be happy or worse, be miserable. God intends to bless everyone irrespective of age, gender, class, or race. But God's blessings are merited and should be worked for. However, no amount of work can measure the blessings of God. God said in *Deuteronomy 30:19, "I call heaven and earth to record this day against you, that I have set before you, life, and death, blessing and curse."* In this passage, God's intention is not to sound rude or hate us but to alert us to know that what we do and how we do it matters. God does not go around looking for those to bless. He goes around blessing those who trust in Him. Whereas Satan, the accuser, is looking for who to lure into a curse because he knows those who follow him will be cursed and destroyed.

Are we not created by one Father? Why should God allow some people to be blessed and some to be cursed? God's blessings take different forms and approaches. The common approach of God's blessing is joy. When good things manifest, your hearts are saturated with the anointing of profound gratitude.

This question is for you to ponder: As you ponder through that question, be kind to ask yourself, am I blessed or cursed? Though it may be hard to answer, you will be able to evaluate your life and evaluate what areas of need in your life should be addressed appropriately through action and deeds.

| 7 |

AUTHORITY OF BLESSINGS

A blessing is God's authority, therefore, an integral part of His plan for you. But there are criteria for God's blessings. His initiative for blessings is dependent upon your relationship with Him. He blessed Noah because of his obedience to His commands and faithfulness in the works of his hands. Abraham was blessed because he obeyed the call and the purpose of God in his life. He was blessed because he served and trusted God with all his heart. David was blessed because he humbled himself to God.

Joseph was blessed and prosperous because he obeyed God's command of not committing adultery, and he humbled himself as a slave and servant to his master and trusted God for deliverance. The blessing of God is the direct reference to our works. God does not act without a cause. The must-be is an effect of work for the cause of blessing to be activated. Blessing is the origin of everything. Without God's blessings, one is doomed. I don't care how much money is sitting in your bank account, or how many assets or housing estates you own in each country, state, or city, or how much life insurance benefits that you have; wealth cannot surpass God's blessings. That's for sure! The blessings of God are continual processes if or when we obey Him.

The opposite of God's blessing is a curse. God's purpose for Man is blessing, but when Man's deeds contradict the purpose of God, the reverse is a curse. God cursed the serpent because he made Adam and Eve violate the command of eating the Tree of Knowledge. Read Genesis 3:14 God was very angry with Eve, so God cursed Eve, and said in verse 16 He said, *"in sorrow thou shall bring forth children."* And finally in *Genesis 3:17, and to the man, God said, cursed be the ground for thy sake, in sorrow shall thou eat of it all the days of thy life.*

THE RELATIONSHIP BETWEEN A BLESSING AND A CURSE IS BY OUR DEEDS, AND THE DIFFERENCE BETWEEN A BLESSING AND A CURSE IS THE AFTERMATH.

God's blessing does not come in one specific form. It could take different routes and forms. They come in abundance with different flavors in the form of money, housing, health, children, employment, recovery from crises, release from prison, justice, child's birth, career, success, or many testimonies. God is like an employer who rewards or gives raises to the most dedicated employees. *"And behold, I come quickly; and my reward is with me, to give every man according as his work shall be."* Revelation 22:12

Everybody in this world has a part to play, and every role is accountable for a reward. The outcome of a blessing is an increase in good health, favor, promotion, appointment, opportunities, joy, hope, and many more. God's blessings indeed come in different ways, and it is also true that they do not come in the ways we expect them to. However, they come in mind-blowing, mouth-wide, jaw-dropping, and wow ways.

As mentioned earlier, the reverse of blessing is curse because it brings failures, disappointments, lack of productivity, poverty, backwardness, illnesses, sorrow, anguish, and torments. God's curse comes in different ways. It can come like an earthquake that disrupts the lands and destroys lives. Many people feel the weight of its impact and damage.

A curse can come like heavy rain, storms, and floods. It can come like fire and burn down all that one has been acquired. It can also come like a plaque and destroy everyone in their household. It can come through a child to terrorize their family's security and safety. It can come like heavy wind and blow off your joy and happiness in a split second. It can come like a unanimous disaster and destroy or disrupt the mind, thoughts, future, children, marriages, families, careers, education, businesses, and wealth. Remember, the curse of Sodom and Gomorrah was because of their deeds and actions. God's rage of anger was because the people's disobedience brought ruin into the City of Sodom and Gomorrah. However, God did not destroy the city until he rescued Lot and his family because they obeyed His command.

In Genesis 19, you can notice Lot's first action was displayed, and in verse 1, he met the two angels, welcomed them into the city, and bowed down to them. After Lot welcomed the two angels, he invited them into his house and fed them. In verse 3, at night, the men in the city demanded Lot to bring out the two men that came to his house, but he refused and implied that they should take his two daughters instead of his guests. Lot tried to plead with them, but they refused. Had they known that the two men were God's messengers, maybe they would have remained calm and gone back. But they insisted that Lot bring out his quests. Since Lot's guests were God's messengers, the angels smote them with blindness. According to Genesis 4:11, every single deed comes with an act of blessing or curse. We can learn from the story of Lot that every day of the week has its blessings and curses. Lot and his family were blessed because of his single act of hospitality, while the other people were cursed with blindness because they harassed God's messengers.

The lesson here is that we should learn to be good and kind to each other, no matter what. Always think positively and pray because each day and hour has its own roadmap for the living. Life is God's command, but living it is an individual's choice. We can choose to live how we want and do what we want and when we want, but we must remember that everything we do and how we choose to live has consequences. The goal of our daily life must remain in the pursuit of God's purpose for our existence.

A Broken Vessel can be Repaired

Adam and Eve brought our brokenness to God. Their sin of disobedience defiled our godly relationship with the Father. But because God is gracious, slow to anger, and abounding in mercy, we have been given the privilege to be repaired and to reunite with God the Father, the Son, and the Holy Spirit through His son, Jesus Christ. Romans 5 reminds us that through one man, sin entered the world, and through the death of Jesus, we are justified by righteousness.

The reason we are broken is because of the deceit of the devil, according to Isaiah 14:14. The angel (Lucifer) was thrown out of Heaven. He was thrown out because of his pride, jealousy, and arrogant thoughts. He wanted to ascend above the heights of the clouds and be like the Highest.

Everything about Lucifer was meant to be perfect until his mind got corrupted, and God saw his mind and threw him into the bottomless dark pit of hell. God created man for a purposeful relationship and for man to multiply and fill the earth. But because of the corrupted mind of the devil, he enticed and lured Eve to disobey God.

The disobedience of one man brought the fall of all men. Satan caused man to fall because of his thirst for power and his plan to gather worshippers for himself. He wanted to build a throne for himself on earth since he could not build one in heaven. No wonder Jesus said, *"Watch and pray so that you may not enter into temptation."* For this very reason, we are bound to pray lest we fall into the trap of Satanic failures and doom. For the purpose of information, Satan is not just one man.

He has many agents because when God sent Angel Gabriel to throw Lucifer out of heaven, he threw him out with his other angelic demons who wanted to help him accomplish his evil plan, Revelation 12:4.

Satan can use anyone, objects, seasons, situations, positions, words, and actions to destroy and oppose God's plans for your life. After all, he used words to convince Eve. So, anything or anybody can serve as an avenue for the devil to use for his ruin. Therefore, we must always be aware of his devices and constantly seek God and pray to Him for our lives. We can and have the power to overcome the devil and his tactics so long as we remain grounded in God's word and pray always.

| 8 |

WHY PRAY?

Have you ever wondered if God is real? Ever asked, if God is in control, why are things getting out of control for you? It is okay to ask, but the truth is that God is real, and God is in control. No matter how much turbulent your life is or how terrible the situation may be, nothing takes God by surprise. Isaiah 55:6-7 says, *"Seek ye the Lord while He may be found, call ye upon him while He is near: Let the wicked forsake his way, and the unrighteous man his thoughts: and let him return unto the Lord, and He will have mercy upon him; and to our God, for He will abundantly pardon."*

The time to let God take control of your situation is now. You must seek the Lord now that the day is still early and bright. God's mercy for Mankind is new every morning, and His faithfulness never fails us. There is a time for everything, a time to find, and a time to have. Sometimes, we get discouraged because we feel that God has failed to answer our requests. But what if I ask you, how long have you sought for the Lord? Seeking the Lord is more than just going to the store to buy milk or juice. Seeking God is waiting on His purpose and believing Him for the things you have not yet seen. Don't wait until the problem is out of hand and you think God is your last resort. Make God first in line, and then take Him on the journey with you from the beginning to find other possibilities.

Seeking God is simply praying to Him. Praying to God is communication to a lovely Father who cannot resist His child's request until it's done. To find a solution to your problem, you must start praying today, not later but NOW. You cannot see a black t-shirt in the darkroom because the t-shirt will blend with the dark. If you must wear a black t-shirt, you must find it during the day. Prayer is not an amusement park where we go to play when we want to. It is an act of daily command that supplies our needs. We need prayer to withstand the thorns in this world. Prayer breaks the seal of temptation and opens the door to victory.

My goal with this book is to explore and share the importance of prayer. *Prayer is an act.* It is a habit that must be learned and maintained. If our prayer life is not managed properly, we can lose it. We are not obligated to pray but mandated to pray. Prayer is a choice. So, we are not under the law to pray. We can choose to pray at will or choose not to pray. Whatever option you choose, it is rightly okay. But remember that prayer is an access to help you overcome every battle. David would not have overcome Goliath without prayer.

Prayer is an integral part of our sustenance. We cannot see the coming of our destiny, but through prayer and the Word of God, the assurance is that our future lies in the hands of God, and whatever the future holds for us, the purpose is for our good and benefit. The world is rapidly changing; we are now in the age of technology. Therefore, we can be assured that our loved ones may be out of sight, but communication is a must if we choose to keep that fire burning. There are many ways of communicating with our loved ones. As the year passes by, there are always new technologies and methods of communication. We got excited when the communication of sending a letter abroad came into existence.

Many years back, our parents sent letters abroad and waited a month for the letter to arrive, and then, wait another month or more to receive feedback. Later, the telephone line came into existence, and then the walkie-talkie, before the invention of the mobile phone. To this day, many of those communication tools are still in existence. These different types of communication came into play because of the need to reach our loved ones quicker from far and near.

Communication is a need that strengthens our relationships with friends, spouses, families, colleagues, neighbors, and loved ones. Without adequate and purposeful communication, there is no healthy and sound relationship. Imagine if you are married or have children and you step out of the house daily without greeting your spouse or communicating with your children about how your day went or ask them, at least, about what they did at school. Your children or spouse will start to wonder what's going on with you and why there is a break in communication. Such households will not trust each other because of a break in communication, breaking trust and relationships.

Lack of communication is a tool of a poor relationship; you cannot live with someone in the same house as a friend or spouse and not communicate effectively. There would be no reason to live together. The need for effective communication is to help deepen our relationships with one another; the more time we spend with friends and families, the deeper our relationships become, the more cordial and trusting partner you build and become.

Prayer is the direct contact line of communicating with God. When Jesus was in heaven with His Father before being sent to earth, it was easy for Him to speak to and with His Father daily physically. A son who sits at the right hand of His Father has more accessible access to communicate at will with Him.

When Jesus came into the world, the path of communicating with God was through prayer, and He showed us a life of prayer in various Biblical instances. Despite Jesus being the Son of God, He still prayed because He was faced with the same pains and tribulations that we face. Jesus came in human flesh, a baby born of a woman. He cried as every other baby would cry. He experienced pain, hunger, thirst, tiredness; he slept, took baths, ate, and suffered abuse, hatred, and even rejection from His people. Jesus grew up like every other kid, and then, when

He began His purpose on earth, He started His mission with prayer. On the account of Jesus beginning His ministry, He fasted and prayed for forty days and forty nights. He was famished on His last day of fasting and prayer; the Holy Spirit took Him to the wilderness where the devil tempted him. Jesus overcame the devil, and the devil's scorn did not prevail *Luke 4:1-12.*

Many people asked why the devil tempted Jesus knowing that He is the son of God? God allowed this event to happen to let us know that Satan does not care about who you are, and He will do anything to trap you into his pit of hell. Satan purposefully knew that Jesus was the Son of God, yet he went to tempt Him. Satan is not at our mercy. He will do anything to derail the purpose of God for our lives. If he could tempt Jesus, who witnessed with His eyes when the angel threw him out from heaven, then, who are we? He can tempt you and everyone on earth. So, for you to overcome Satan's schemes, you must stay strong in God and pray diligently. The only way to build our relationship with God is through prayer. After all, it is the most reliable form of communicating with God the Father, Son, and the Holy Spirit.

Prayer unravels the purpose of God in our lives and directs our paths to light. There is a thin line between light and darkness. The light is the spiritual power of the supernatural thing that the naked eye cannot see. The reality of the outstanding is the spirit and truth of worshipping God and believing in the saving grace of our Creator. Darkness is the spiritual control force of the hidden thing that the naked eyes cannot see. Still, it endangers our minds into a falsehood spirit of calloused thought, lust, and wickedness that prevails out of the unseen realm of the darkest pit, and only through the power of prayer can we prevail.

| 9 |

PRAYER: CHANGE AGENT

Prayer does not only change us, but it changes our situations. If God is not involved, there is no better way. Your prayer can change any situation. During one of my communications with a woman, our conversation led to something unexpected and unimaginable. Instantly, she poured out her heart about her only son. She told me that her son is a brilliant college student, but he became involved with bad friends that derailed him from pursuing his dreams of becoming a medical doctor. As a mother, she became fed up with her son's irresponsible behavior and even wished that she never had him as her son. When her son continued with his recklessness, she disowned him and banned him from their home.

I felt so sorry for her, listening to her troubles. My heartbeat raised as I imagined what she was going through. I didn't have much to tell her. So, I asked her how often she prayed. "Not anymore. I am tired of praying. That thing called prayer doesn't work. Also, I don't even care about God anymore. He does not yield any crops no matter how we feel disconnected with our children," she lamented. The heart of a mother is still on her child. When she was done expressing herself to me, I suggested that she starts praying for her son. I promised her that God would surely make a difference in his life.

God gives us children as a reward of His love. Not necessarily our biological children, but all children far and near. I encouraged the woman to pray and wait patiently on God's plan and purpose. Approximately six months later, she came back to me and said that she had good news. I was very excited and all ears to hear. "Roseline, I am only telling you of my favor from God because you encouraged me to trust in God and inspired me to know that there is nothing God cannot do. You were aware of my troubles and worries. Now, it's time for my testimony. Last night, my son walked into my bedroom and told me that he had been accepted into a pre-med program. I couldn't believe it until he showed me the admission acceptance letter. My heart was full. I jumped up and thought about you because you encouraged me to pray for my son and not give up on him."

Prayer is not magic. However, most people think that prayer is magic. What makes prayer seem like magic is because the supposedly impossible situation is made possible. The magic of prayer is its testimonies. Without prayer, there are no possibilities. Prayer is very vital in our daily lives. Prayer is the direct phone number to God, and His response to our requests is straightforward and timely. We cannot make a difference without changing our thoughts and perceptions. When you go to God in prayer, He will change your worst story to the best story ever!

The most important aspect of prayer is prayer as a change agent. Abraham became the Father of the nation through faith and righteousness. Faith and righteousness go together with prayer. Prayer brings faith, and faith brings hope, and hope, expectations. The Word of God in Proverbs 23:3 says, *"that let not thine heart envy sinners but be thou in the fear of the Lord all day long. For there is an end"*; *"the expectation of the righteous shall not be cut off"* according to Proverbs 10:24.

God understands your needs, but He wants you to bring your request to Him. God knows that you have an expectation for your future, your children, and your family. However, there are some manifested spiritual forces that hinder your expectations from realization. But when you cling to God in prayer and fasting, the God of miracles will work to expose the enemy and bring you to victory. The Word of God in Matthew 6:8 says, *"be not ye, therefore, like unto them: for your Father knoweth what things ye have need of, before ye ask."* There is nothing that you will ask that your Father in heaven does not know already, yet He wants you to pray because that is one of the ways God can build your relationship with Him and work in your favor of needs.

Esther is an excellent practical example of how prayer is a game-changer. According to Esther 6:1-12: God does not negotiate with your situations; He gives commands of what should be done, and they will be so. Esther could not have gone to the king without prior approval from the king for her to come into the kings' chamber. But through prayer, the case was different, and the game changed hands. Esther no longer requested to make the order, but she gave a command, and the king granted her wish.

| 10 |

WHAT PRAYER DOES

Prayer is a facet of cleansing, change, acceptance, breakthrough, healing, provision, assistance, peace, comfort, courage, and personal relationship with God. Did you know that the most important thing that prayer does is cleansing? Prayer nurtures your spiritual growth and revitalizes your soul. The spirit, mind, and body must come together in submission to the Holy Spirit in thanksgiving and supplication for prayer to effect its purpose.

When you bring yourself to God in prayer, God will draw you closer to Himself, and He will forgive your past and present mistakes. He will then purify your life for freshness and renewal of His divine covenant. The mercy of God is forgiving, and His love lasts forever. God is Holy, and they that worship Him must worship in spirit and truth; thus, they must be holy in His presence. When you bring yourself to prayer, God will cleanse you off spiritual dirt that will stand in your way of His relationship with God. In as much as God wants our relationship with Him, He certainly does not want you to befriend Him with dirt and filthiness.

Prayer is an instrument of change; when we pray, God will direct His thoughts and purpose to us, and He will send the Holy Spirit to remind us to stay out of sin. Sin is spiritual dirt that hinders our relationship with God. God knows that we are sinners because out of sin, we were born. So, God is not in place to judge us, but in place to cleanse us from our sins to accept our friendship, no matter the magnitude of our past wrongs. 2 *Timothy 3:16 says, "All scripture is given by inspiration of God, and is profitable for doctrine, for reproof, for correction, for instruction in righteousness:"*

When we pray, the revelation of the Word of God will teach us in the direction of His Light, and through prayer, God will correct us from our wrong, and through prayer, God will rebuke the devil and his agents, and through prayer, God will instruct us on the right things. Prayer is not a material want that we walk into the store to buy. Prayer is a spiritual need that must be applied daily in our lives; otherwise, the devil will use us at his disposal for his pleasure and destruction. I pray that the devil will have no place in our lives. Amen.

There is a tendency for committing sin knowingly and unknowingly. Sin is an abomination in the eyes of God. The reason why our relationship is impeded from God is sin. We are prone to temptations, and we cannot resist the temptations if we do not pray. One of the major reasons why our prayers are not answered is because of our sins. *Isaiah 59:2, "says our iniquities have separated us from God."* Sin is prevalent in our weakness and weakness to our spiritual being. Jesus said, "pray, lest ye fall into temptation." Satan is always in our way to tempt us into doing evil. *Mark 14:38, "Watch ye and pray, lest ye enter into temptation. The spirit truly is ready, but the flesh is weak."*

God knows our weaknesses, and He is always here to help us turn them into strengths. The flesh is the weakest part of humans. It is the lust of the flesh that causes us to fall. Adam and Eve fell because of the lust of the flesh. They wanted to gain more knowledge from what God had given them. This caused them to fall, and since then, we have become prone to falling into temptations. Sin is accountable to every man, but by the blood of Jesus, we are set free from the slavery of sin. I pray that God will give us new hearts to refrain from our old ways so that our prayers will not be in vain.

Prayer allows us to accept and leave what we cannot change for God and accept His will even in trials and temptations. The will of God is perfect, but most time, it is hard to accept the will of God. But when we earnestly pray, God's will and purpose for us will become more apparent and undoubtful; knowing that God is in control

Without Prayer, there is no breakthrough. The best therapy that anyone can ask for in any situation is prayer. Read James 5:12-18, when you pray, there is assurance that God has heard you, and He will answer you unexpectedly. Consistent prayer revives our souls and rejuvenates our spirits. When we pray, there is a tendency for joy that tells us that God has already made a way.

Everyone needs healing. Healing wears many hats, and it takes many approaches. Naaman, a prominent man in the bible, struggled with healing until he met Elisa, and God healed his leprosy. Sometimes, we underestimate the power of supernatural healing. The name of Jesus is stronger than any tower and mightier than any power. There is healing in the name of Jesus, and at the mention of the name of Jesus, every knee must bow, and every tongue will confess that Jesus is Lord.

When you are faced with a situation that you cannot handle, let God do it for you. Surrender your situation to God, and let His power perform the miracle. If there is any area in your life that needs healing from sickness, heartbreak, financial crises, loss of a family member, loss of home, loss of a spouse, loss of a child, loss of benefits, and loss of privileges, this is the time to commit to God. Call the name of Jesus over your situations and proclaim restoration over your life. Don't underestimate the power of your tongue.

Did you know your tongue is capable of setting you free? When you declare Jesus as your Lord of lords, and the Kings above kings on Earth, and the warrior over all giants, He will make Himself manifest. Out of the heart, the mouth speaks. If you receive Jesus in your heart, your declaration of healing will manifest in your life.

Getting into the habit of praying is the best way to know what prayer does. Most importantly, prayer is an immediate need that sustains our lives. Jesus commands us to pray. He also taught us how to pray and told us to always flee from temptation. He said when we pray in secret, His father will reward us openly. When you pray to God, pray with confidence because God will hear and answer your prayers.

| 11 |

PRAYER CHANGES CIRCUMSTANCES

Worried about your problems? There is only one way out. *"David said I sought the Lord, and He heard me and delivered me from all my fears."* Psalm 34:4. No matter your situation, there is a Higher power that can reverse that situation. No matter the magnitude of your circumstance, your prayer can change for good. Prayer to change your situation requires faith and patience. There is a difference between the circumstance of a Christ believer and a non-Christ believer. God knows that we are in the world of temptations, and certainly, He will not let you walk on the trial path alone, read 1 Corinthians 10:13.

There is no one without a circumstance or situation and no circumstance without a solution. The best approach to solving a problem is letting peace reign in your heart. It sounds odd to think why you should have peace when facing a terrible circumstance, right? It's not odd to believers. The powerful tool of prayer is peace. The peace of God that surpasses all human understanding is the key that will energize you to take the authority to solve any situation. Philippians 4:6-7, *"Be careful about nothing; but in everything by prayer and supplication with thanksgiving, let your requests be made known unto God. And the peace of God, which passeth all understanding, shall keep your hearts and minds through Christ Jesus."*

When you are faced with strange circumstances, the one thing that the circumstances will do is rob your mind away from peace and then cause you to become angry with everything and anyone. When you draw yourself to prayer in silence, the Holy Spirit who sees your trial and temptations will have mercy on you and show you another way out to victory, according to 1 John 5:4.

Often, people ask if God created us, why then do we have to pray? Prayer to God is obedience to His commands. God desires for us to have a relationship with Him. He is in love with us. If we surrender to His will, He will beckon us to Himself. The will of God is for us to live happily and joyfully, but what happens if you are the stumbling block to your happiness? God is the master of the universe; the moon and the stars shine at His commands.

He said, choose ye this day, life and death. If you choose life, you will live abundantly beyond human imagination. You cannot command the moon to stand; neither can you command the rain to fall. Everything happens at the command of God's voice. If you obey the will of God, He will command the inhabitants of the earth to favor you. *Luke 18:27 says,- "and he said, The things which are impossible with men are possible with God.*

| 12 |

PRAY WITH FAITH

A prayer without faith is like taking a shower without soap. Faith means to wait and stand firm in the truth of God's Words and His prophecies in the Bible for your life, unwavering and unshaken, knowing that God is an ever-moving God. He moves with purpose, a Changer who changes everything, and a builder who rebuilds what was cast away.

Often, situations will challenge your faith, leaving you with no choice but to do otherwise because of the situation's urgency. Usually, your faith will waver, thoughts will fail you, and your spiritual belief could get twisted because you feel God is not there to save you. This is the time to lift your spirit and mind closer to God because, in the toughest of times, His Spirit is made manifest when you have faith in Him. Trials and struggles can make you feel obscure. It is then that you cling to the Word of God and prayer. Faith is like a seed; when you water the seed daily, it will grow and bloom. The more you pray, the more your faith grows.

Isaiah 40:31 tells us that God strengthens us during our time of waiting. Like a waiter at a restaurant. Waiting on someone is to serve the person. Your faith will drive your hope, and hope carries you to believe in God. The devil is a scam with many agents to rage war against the children of God. The purpose of Satan is to frustrate you, and God's greater plan is to dispose of them. Prayer of faith is an assurance to take over what was lost in your life through the storm of challenges.

Challenges come to disrupt your mind and sweep your feet away from the truth of God's Word and feed you the lies and condemnation of the devil. I can tell you now, don't be shaken, stand firm with the truth, have faith in God, and your victory is around the corner. *Psalm 34:18, " The Lord is near to the brokenhearted and saves the crushed in spirit."* Mordecai could have been swift off with the pranks and boast of Haman, but his faith in God and prayer turned the story of Haman's boat to failure, and Mordecai's story became the headline of honor and victory. Esther made a resolve to obey the commands of God and was ready to die for her decision according to Esther 4:15-16. God does not only hear our prayers; he also honors our prayers and grants our requests.

The only way to nurture your faith is through prayer and studying the Word of God. We can understand that even the disciples of Jesus trembled and were shaken in their faith upon Jesus being with them because the human mind is full of doubts. With the carnal mind and human imagination, it is impossible to walk on water. Jesus called Peter to come to the other side where He was; he feared to walk because, in the history of humanity, no one ever walked on water except by being inside a canoe or boat. But Jesus knew that only faith could turn the impossible to possible if we believe. Read Matthew 14:22-33: although Peter walked on water, but his faith wavered when the heavy wind came, and Peter began to sink. He called on Jesus to save him. Jesus knows that you have human flesh; that's why He is always on time to save you if you have faith.

Faith is the mother of belief. With faith, you can do anything. Jesus said in Matthew 17:20, *"...If you have faith as a grain of mustard seed, ye shall say unto this mountain, Remove hence to yonder place; and it shall remove; and nothing shall be impossible unto you."* Making something happen from the ordinary is a great accomplishment that is not common but possible because the anointing of faith to move mountains is granted unto you.

Faith is your authority, to declare and it will stand. Elijah declared by faith that it would not rain for three years, and God granted him the request by faith because Elijah stood on God's Words, and he acted on faith, and through faith, there was no rainfall for three days according to 1 Kings 17. Faith requires you to wait patiently on God, as David exclaimed in Psalm 40:1. If you must pray, you must wait. God's time is the best, and the best comes with laughter and joy. God does not act on our timing but His. He does not forsake those who pray to Him and wait on Him. Sooner or later, He will come to your rescue.

Prayer with faith directs you to know that God has heard your cry and answered you. When you are praying, you are standing on the solid rock. That solid rock is Jesus, according to 1 Corinthians 10:4. Sometimes, God delays answering your prayer to test your faith in Him. Read 2 Peter 3:9; If you have not fully repented, God can withhold His answers to your prayer for you to repent fully. Any challenge, situation, or mishap is a trial to test your faith. When you stand the test of this present time, you will win the crown of victory, and those that laughed first will laugh last, read James 1:12.

The purpose of prayer is to grow our relationship with God. The act of intimacy is commitment and communication. Many relationships struggle because of the lack of commitment and communication. When commitment is out of sight, the relationship is ruined, and when communication is not involved, the danger is far beyond imagination. Commitment and communication work together. God is so interested in our commitment and communication with Him.

Infact, the best way for God to communicate with us is through His Word, prayers, dreams, and revelations. God will not come down from heaven to communicate with you, but reading the Bible and prayer will yield the foundation of communicating with God. Faith is the foundation as a true Christian, and without faith, you cannot get through the toughest of times, and without faith, there is no commitment, no expectation, and no outcome. We are born to pray constantly because Satan has defiled the earth, and without prayer, Satan will have his way to estrange every step of your happiness

Prayer is your strength, and prayer unravels your fortune. So, developing your prayer habit or prayer life is an essential work that has to do with hearing the Word of God. Read Romans 10:17, everything that happened in the Bible was real. as it was then so it is now that our faith determines how we hear and communicate with God. We can accept that these things happened by faith, and through faith, the will and plan of God for us will manifest. God called Abram to go to a place, a place with no direction or zip code. He rose with his family and began a trip without an address of where they were going; Abram knew that God does not come into our lives without a purpose. He could not have wanted to go; after all, he was old and didn't have much strength to walk to his destination, but he accepted the plan of God and began a walk by faith. *"By faith Abraham, when he was called to go out into a place which he should after receive for an inheritance, obeyed; and he went out, not knowing whither he went."* Hebrew 11:8. A prayer of faith is a walk of transformation and restoration. Because God adores your prayer for that reason, God will perform wonders that would open your mouths wide in the congregation of friends and families.

| 13 |

PRAY WITH HUMILITY

Humility is a virtue. It is the most form of claiming your victory and taking over. *"The fear of the Lord is the beginning of knowledge..."* Proverbs 1:7. God is not a ghost that we should fear, but a Spirit to adore and tremble when we approach Him. Prayer is not for the wise but for the humble. If you must receive, you must be ready to humble yourself in the presence of the Lord to receive His precious gift.

Respect is an attitude. The attitude we demonstrate to our fellow humans can promote us or degrade us. It will be very disrespectful for you to walk into the CEO's office at your job and demand a vacation approval without a prior request to see him or her. As humans, we have a way of getting something when we need to have it. But when it comes to our relationship with God, it is totally different. God does not look at our facial appearances or expressions to see if we are faking being friendly or happy with each other. Instead, He looks into our hearts and rewards us based on what's in our hearts. *Jeremiah 17:10, "I the Lord search the heart, I try the reins, even to give every man according to his ways, and according to the fruit of his doings."*

When we go to God in prayer, there is a condition that must be adhered to; humility. According to James 4:10, we are to humble ourselves in the sight of the Lord. There is always a reward for the humble.

Being humble means foolish in the eyes of Man. But in the sight of God, being humble means wisdom. The reason why God rejects the prayers of many is because of their pride and arrogant mindset. Read James 4:3.

There is a difference between relating with God and Man. God cannot be fooled or tricked. He does not move towards the sinner but withdraws from the sinner. God does not favor the sinner but the righteous. Read 1 Peter 3:2 NIV, "when they see the purity and reverence of your lives." God's eyes are on you. He sees your pain, torment, rejection, abandonment, frustration, and accusation. God can do what Man cannot do. Just be patient and wait on Him. It may tarry, but He will surely get you out of the deep mire. It may seem that God isn't near to you, but He sure is working on your behalf behind the scenes until His glory is seen by all in His time. When challenges do not consume you, God's glory is manifesting on your behalf. Just stand firm, humble yourself, and be diligent in deeds and words. Sooner or later, eyes will see, and the ears will hear the glory of God's mighty works in your life. *"But as it is written, Eye hath not seen, nor ear heard, neither have entered into the heart of man, the things which God hath prepared for them that love him." 1 Corinthians 2:9.*

The wicked pride and boast about his deeds, but how well does he know that both knowledge and wisdom come from God? The iniquities of the wicked have separated them from God, and sooner or later, the end shall be justified. *Isaiah 59:2, says "But your iniquities have separated between you and your God, and your sins have hid his face from you, that he will not hear."*

The fool says there is no God. Man's heart is full of foolishness, deceit, and mockery. For instance, urging to cheat the poor to heap up wealth and status for themselves. Their pride of cheating the poor has overblown them into the bottomless pit of greed and destruction. Sooner or later, the same coin shall be poured back to them, more than the measure they did unto others because God cannot be deceived or mocked. He has a way of paying everyone back with the same coin. *"For with what judgment ye judge, ye shall be judged: and with what measure ye mete, it shall be measured to you again." Matthew 7:2*

| 14 |

PRAY TO RECEIVE NOT TO GRUMBLE

The essence of asking is to receive. *"And all things, whatsoever ye shall ask in prayer, believing, ye shall receive." Matthew 21:22* We seem to give up easily most times because we expect to receive in a specific way or pattern that we expected or wished. God does not grant us selfish responses, neither does He neglect our specific needs. God sees all things and the heart of Man. He knows our needs. God's time is not our time, but He certainly understands our needs and grants us what's best for us. *"Behold the fowls of the air: for they sow not, neither do they reap, nor gather into barns; yet your heavenly Father feedeth them. Are ye not much better than they?" Matthew 6:26.*

God knows what is good and bad for us. He is God after all. If and when He does not grant us what we want does not mean that He does not care about us or our needs or has neglected our request. But He is certainly working in our favor to give us the best. God is like our earthly father, who will not give his child an expensive phone or the car of their choice just because the child only wishes to have that car or phone (for instance) because it is trending or because all their friends own that. God does not grant us a selfish desire, just for what we want. But He gives us what we need for the best and a lifetime. God is a good

Father, the Father who understands His children's needs, and a Father that never disappoints.

God took the Israelites from Egypt to the land that He promised to give to them. When God brought Israelites to the wilderness, a place for them to rest until He established His plans for them to move and take over the Land of Canaan. The Israelites were grumbling and making strong demands. God provided all their needs, shielded them, and loved them more than any other nation. Yet, they were not satisfied with what they had. So, God commanded Moses to choose 12 spies to go and survey the land of milk and honey that He would give to them. For instance, what is the soil of that fruitful land like? The spies went as instructed.

When they came back, they came with a report of how fortified the land was, and then, they said, "but the people in that land are powerful." This caused the Israelites to grumble more and wish they had died in Egypt instead of coming out to die in the wilderness. God was furious at their murmurings and grumblings despite all the signs and wonders He had shown them. So, God planned to strike them with a plaque, but Moses pleaded with God and requested His mercy and forgiveness. God heard Moses's request to preserve them. Though He forgave them, He said, because they grumbled and disobeyed Him, all those who saw His signs and wonders in Egypt will not see the promise land according to Numbers 14:22-23.

The Israelites disobeyed God and murmured over all the good things that God planned for them. God was angry, so He denied them from seeing the promise land of Canaan because of their ingratitude. When you pray, do not grumble. Ask instead. Most people use prayer to question God. For example, God, are you really God? If you are God, why am I still living in a wretched house like this? I can't even afford to buy a television or pay for internet or cable service. Some will ask, 'God, why are you still letting me live after all these troubles?' and wonder why they are still living. These types of prayers withdraw your benefits from God.

Every Christian or child of God is entitled to God's kingdom benefits. One of the benefits of God for you is to live a life of worthiness and fruitfulness. The source of everything is from God. No matter how we run, without God making a way for our efforts to be realized, our race is meaningless. Learn to appreciate God in any circumstance, whether good or bad. Being thankful for the creation of God in your life is for a purpose. Be generous with your prayer. Give an offering of praise and worship to God. Sing songs to praise Him for His love in your life. David said, *"because thy love is better than my life, my lips shall praise thee." Psalm 63:3*

Life is more worthy than anything. No matter the situation, God's love shall prevail. Things will fall apart from you. People may reject you or turn against you. Friends may hate you, and affliction may arise from nowhere. You may be faced with financial issues, incidents, or accidents that will derail or disable your plans. Nevertheless, God will never forsake you.

When your mind is fixed on God and Jesus, the road map will be clear. David was faced with various forms of war, yet his mind never second-guessed him if God was there to help him? He lived his days with God. Though he committed many sins in the sight of God, he was quick to find himself guilty and pleaded to God for forgiveness. As a child of God, we must ask to receive and not grumble. No matter how bad your situation is, be still and know that God will walk you through it. Read Psalm 23:1. If not for your love, where would I be?

| 15 |

PRAYER CHANGES DESTINIES

God determines our destinies. There is no one without a destiny. It is our choice to groom our destiny or destroy it. God has predetermined His hidden counsel and plans for us. He said to us in Jeremiah 1:5, *"Before I formed you in your mothers' belly, I knew you."* God also said in Jeremiah 29:11, *"For I know the plans I have for you."* God's plans are clear and direct. He wants us to have good lives and work in the abundance of joy and happiness on earth.

Prayer is communication to God in our relationship with Him. Prayer is also an appeal or request to our dear and loving Father, whose plans and purpose are to ask for anything, and it shall be done for us. God wants us to be open in our communications with Him and be free to tell Him everything and anything. Though He is already aware of our thoughts, dreams, and plans when you tell Him, we are reverencing His sovereignty and adoring Him as the author and the finisher of everything.

God designed our destinies, and He has already predestined us for what He wants us to be. His declaration and decrement are certain. Did we also know that God can add more bright colors into our destinies if we genuinely seek Him and ask Him to change the ugly parts of our destinies?

Most people say that God's plans are inevitable. Yes, I agree to some extent. However, God can delay our destines or hasten our destinies. God has the final say in our lives. There are certain things that God has declared and decreed to happen in our lives that will happen, no matter what. One out of thousands of God's plans for us that are inevitable is death. No child of God will die untimely. Death is a sure process for every man, but certain guidelines from God would prevent us from dying until the plans and purpose for God in our lives are manifested. Until all His plans for us are manifested, the old age of Elijah will be bestowed on us.

Prayer and supplication can change our destinies. Our destiny is our destination in life. Life is a vehicle, and everyone on earth is riding in one vehicle. God is the driver that drives our lives. In this God's vehicle, everyone, including the poor, rich, young, and old, ride inside this one vehicle. However, some people get discouraged and decide to get down from the vehicle because the journey is taking too far. At the same time, some choose not to ride anymore because they found a shorter route. Some remain in the vehicle no matter how long it takes because they are patient and courageous and determined to ride to the end of the journey. Life is a vehicle of perseverance and courage. No wonder God said in *James 1:12*, *"Blessed is the man who remains steadfast under trial, for when he has stood the test he will receive the crown of life, which God has promised to those who love him."*

God is a game-changer, a promise fulfiller, a renewal of birthright, and a way maker. The road may be too far to travel but be rest assured that He controls the steering. So, we need to be more patient and trust God. He never disappoints. There was a gentleman in the Bible called Jabez. The Hebrew word for Jabez means "sorrow." His mother gave birth to him in pain. So, because of that ignorance and lack of spiritual discernment, his mother named him Jabez because she had him out of painful labor and sorrow. Jabez grew up and understood the meaning of his name. Knowing that this name could cause a dread of destiny, he decided to take matters of his mind to God. Jabez prayed to God, and God heard his request according to 1 Chronicles 4:9-10.

One day, I talked to some people about God's marvelous works and faithfulness to man, and someone asked if God is faithful, why did he destroy Sodom and Gomorrah? God is a God of purpose; He does His things purposefully and timely. Before God destroyed Sodom and Gomorrah, He gave them time to repent. Abraham asked God, *"if you find ten people who are righteous, will you still destroy the land?"* and God responded, *"if I find ten people, "I will spare the land for their sake."* Genesis 18:20-33.

Repentance is God's glory. It gladdens God to see us repent because we benefit from being the kings and queens of Heavenly emancipation when we repent. Jesus said, *"in my fathers' house there are many mansions."* John 14:2. God's plans and purpose are for us to be a part of His glorious Kingdom in Heaven's abode.

God's plan for your destiny is as simple as ABCDEFG
A-Accept God's plan and purpose for your life
B-Become part of the glorious heavenly kingdom
C-Communicate and commit to God
D-Depart from evil
E-Enjoy the benefits of God's presence
F-From age to age, God never changes
G-God's purpose is for you to prosper

God's design for our DNA is to live a life of worthiness, increase, an abundance of joy, and fruitfulness. Are there things that can mismatch our DNAs? Yes, disobedience and sin can cause DNA mutation in our destinies. However, God is the Maker of our DNA; therefore, He has the power to correct a damaged DNA or destiny and tune us back towards the direction of His perfect will for us.

God promised the Israelites a land filled with milk and honey. In Numbers 14:8, the Israelites' ignorance and disobedience made God change His plans of taking them to Canaan, and their future was destroyed in the Wilderness. Callousness and ignorance are the misconceptions of the mind that mislead us from God's directions and purpose for us. Because of the Israelites' callousness, doubt, disobedience, and fear, they missed the promised land that God had planned for their wellbeing, and they wandered aimlessly in the wilderness, forgoing the abundance of "milk and honey."

God told them that for 40 days and 40 nights, all the people who saw the wonders of God in Egypt would not see the promised land until they were all dead, except Joshua and Caleb because they believed that God's Word does not fail. Their faith and trust kept them alive, and they went with the younger generation into Canaan, read Numbers 14:26-35. The initial plan for the Israelites after God brought them out of Egypt was to grant them a Land of Canaan, filled with milk and honey, but God decided to change that plan of destiny that He had in mind for them to their own coin of destiny that they declared.

Prayer can change your destiny but be mindful that every word the Israelites spoke was a prayer to God. It was their lamentation and outcry in Egypt that God heard, and then, He chose Moses, His servant, to go and deliver them from Egypt. When they got to the wilderness, about the time for God to settle them in a fortified land, they lamented again; crying and wishing they died in Egypt or the wilderness, instead of dying in a strange land by the sword. Numbers 14:2. God was furious and wanted to destroy them, but Moses pleaded to God to forgive their rebellion. God replied, "I have forgiven them as you asked Moses; nevertheless, I will pay them back in the coin that they wished for themselves. God declared to them, *"as you have spoken in my ears, so I will do for you." Number* 14:28.

Can you imagine how the Israelites used their own hands to rob themselves of the full benefit of unlimited blessings that God had for them? Be patient and trust God. God is not a wicked Master. He is a meek and gentle Father who considers us for His good plans and purposes and gives us many opportunities to repent, excel, and enjoy the fruits of our labor.

God is a graceful protector of our lives; His grace and protection binds us together to keep us from evil. Every hair strand on our heads is numbered, and God will not allow it to fall without His permission. You are the child of God's bright destiny. Nothing can endanger your life and take you away from the will of God as long as your faith is in Him. When God's marvelousness is poured on you, even Satan will become fearful of you because God has appointed you for Himself. The road may be rocky, sleek, or rough, but hold firmly to Him, and the ride will be smoother and joyous.

Job was a faithful servant of God. He appointed Job to Himself and bestowed him with honor and wealth. One day, Satan went to God while God's sons went to present themselves to Him. God asked Satan, *"have you seen Job, my servant, how upright he has been?"* Satan answered, *"well, Job is serving you diligently because, God, you have blessed him so much with all the riches."* Then Satan asked, let me try Job and see if he will still serve you; God permitted Satan to inflict Job with pain and anguish to test his faith. When Satan saw that Job remained faithful to God, Satan ran away, and God restored all that Job had lost, and God doubled the portions of Job's blessings, and Job was blessed more than what he had before. Job 42:12.

Our destinies are in God's hands, and His good plans for us cannot be realized if we don't trust in Him and always pray daily. Don't be alarmed by the story of Job or get scared thinking that God will allow Satan to inflict you with sorrows and torment. Many people ask why God allowed Job to suffer so much. He allowed this story to exist for us to learn something extensive from it. We should know that if we are chosen, we must be worthy to receive health and wealth in abundance, but the way of victory is rocky. Only those who can withstand the rain and fire will merit the crown of Joy.

While I was studying the story of Job, I drew many inferences from the climax. Below is the summary from the story of Job.

1. Job was a man of faith
2. God trusted that Job would not fail
3. Satan was ashamed
4. God blessed Job more than ever

Always remember that your destiny is in God's hands and that He has the final say. What He says will surely come to pass. No matter the challenges, your destiny lies in God's hands.

Prayer: *Heavenly Father, I believe you are the God of all possibilities, and all power and majesty belong to you. Lord, please grant me the strength to trust in you, help me know that when all doors close, there is another door you will set for me. Lord, please, help me to depend on you always. Amen.*

| 16 |

PRAYER TURNS LIFE BATTLES INTO BLESSINGS

Life is a battle. The moment a child is born, the most important thing the midwife or the healthcare provider expects to happen is to hear the child cry. If the child does not cry, it indicates that something is wrong, and the child could be in danger. For this reason, all efforts must be made to make sure that the child cries.

While we are on earth, we are on the battlefield. Therefore, whether we like it or not, we must fight. But not all who fight will win. Winning is from the Lord. Every day, we are running and fighting with eventful moments of ups and downs, unexpected circumstances, unplanned bills, missed opportunities, illnesses, poverty, storms, unemployment, addictions, natural disasters, and so on. Sometimes, we feel discouraged, and we ask, "when will this be over?" The truth is, when you know that God is working in your favor, you will realize that no matter the battle that you are facing, you are on the winning side.

Our bodies are unique aspects of God's glory. But why then do we face vigorous battles? God's purpose for us was to fill the earth with good things and for us to enjoy the benefits of His daily blessings. God did not create us to fight life battles, but our ancestors and our first father and mother of the earth chose this battle for us. So, the only way that we can break that yoke of battle is through prayer.

God created Man and put him in the Garden of Eden, and He clearly warned him not to eat the tree of knowledge. God also told him to feel free to eat any other tree, except that one tree. We are deliberately faced with the issue of doing something that we know we shouldn't do. Still, we become selfish and ignorant because we want to experiment to see what the outcome will be like, or we want to see if there are really any consequences. Most of the time, it's not because we like to do it, but pride makes us stubborn, and we become victims.

After God had strictly instructed and warned Man, then God created Eve. God expected Adam to take Eve on a tour of the garden and show her around. He expected him to tell Eve the rules that God gave him, which I certainly believe Adam did give Eve all the instructions from God. Until Satan ruined their stay in the beautiful garden by deceiving Eve and putting everyone into the mess of sin. Lucifer, the Satan, is a prideful man; the foundation of his fall was pride and arrogance, according to Isaiah 14:12-15.

After Satan was thrown down, at God's appointed time, God formed Man. Therefore, Satan, whose only desire was/is to compete with God, tricked Eve, the first mother of the earth, to eat from the forbidden tree. Eve's disobedience made her fall short of the glory of God. Eve gave the fruit of the tree to Adam, and the consequences of this act brought life battles to us all. Genesis 3:1-7. Satan fought to devour the promise of God for Mankind because the Garden of Eden was His territory and because God barred him from it and terminated his angelic and heavenly privileges and assignments. So, Satan vowed to draw everyone he can to him, torment them, and leave them in anguish. Ezekiel 28:13-18.

The pride of Satan brought down his fall from Heaven, and since then, he fought to bring the fall of Man. Since Satan introduced the tree of knowledge to Mankind, battle, death, missed marriages, financial struggles, education backwardness, career disappointment, children's enemy, child abuse, child death, terrorism, sexual abuses, unending wars, health disparities, race discriminations, segregation, poverty, co-worker oppositions, murders, suicides, and household enemy have become the battles of life.

The life battle of everyone is not the same; Mr. A may have a battle of financial issues. Mr. B may have a battle of unemployment, and Mr. C may be faced with wrong accusations or child abuse, and so on. But no matter how little or big the struggle may seem, it is still a battle, and our hearts will be disturbed until the battles are over.

No one person is free from life's battle. Everyone has their varied areas of battles. One may be affluent but may be faced with marital issues, mental illness, or suicidal thoughts. While another may be illness-free but he or she may be dealing with discrimination and prejudices. The other may be rich and illness-free, but dealing with opposition of different family attack that runs in the family. Everyone has their own coin of battle. I always ask my friends, "if you think where you are is worst, wait until another person tells you his or her story, and then, you will have a choice to decide where you would prefer to be."

One of my friends once told me that she wished she was born into a wealthy family where she would not have to worry about money. I replied to her and said, "show me a person without a problem, and I will tell you he or she was not born from a woman." I am not trying to say that the cause of our problems is from a woman, but I am simply saying that our first parents adulterated the foundation of life-free battle that God had planned for us when they disobeyed God and ate the forbidden fruit.

I often say that a true father is always on time to answer his children's calls. God is our true Father, and He is always in place and on time to hear us when we call on Him. The only approach to fight the battles of life is to turn our weakness to God's glory. Battles will come to persuade us, but our response is what makes the difference. David said, *"though a host should encamp against me, my heart shall not fear"* Psalm 27:3.

Apostle Paul said, *"in everything give thanks, for this is the will of God in Christ Jesus for you"* 1 Thessalonians 5:18.

When we are faced with battles, there is a tendency to be weak, tired, frail, and even give up. Would God want you to go through this torment? No! Only the chosen will be set free. God loves everyone, but love is about give and take. You cannot take what you don't have. No one plants a seed of cucumber and harvests strawberries. You only harvest what you planted.

When your heart is fixed on God, He will not let you drown in that deep ocean. He will provide you with unquenchable energy, no matter the hit or heat of the battle. Paul said, *"three times I pleaded to the Lord to take this thorn away from me, and the Lord said, "My grace is sufficient for you, for my power is made perfect in your weakness"* 2 Corinthians 12:8-9.

God does not forsake His people, neither does He allow the righteous to perish with the wicked. His ways are not our ways. Sooner or later, your battles will turn to blessings only if you decide to follow Him and allow Him to carry your burdens for you. Many people say, "it is what it is, it was meant to be, God has planned for it, and there is nothing anyone can do about it." I beg to differ. I am fascinated with the story of Hezekiah, and each time I read it, my jaws will drop, and I'm amazed at the wonders and magnificent performance of God in his life.

The earth is not our home. It's a temporary residence, and one day, we will all be dancing and singing with the angels in heaven. God has granted everlasting life to all who serve Him, but He also has the call of glory to His people at the appointed time. God wants us to live a worthy life until old age, where we will sit with our loved ones and enjoy the fruits of the land.

One day, God sent Prophet Isaiah to tell Hezekiah to prepare his house for it was time for him to be called home and be with the Lord. Hezekiah heard the message, turned to the wall, and prayed to God to remember all his diligent services. Hezekiah laid his prayer request to God, and he was assured that God has heard his request. Later, God sent back the prophet to tell Hezekiah that He had heard his plea and accepted him. God added another 15 years to his age and promised to deliver Hezekiah and his city from the battles of King Assyria in Isaiah 38:4-6.

Notice how God did not only answer the request of Hezekiah, but He also fought his battles. God is a God of double blessings. When you ask for one, He will add many to your bosom. Hannah asked for a child, but God gave her Samuel the Prophet, and God granted her three more sons and two daughters.

| 17 |

PRAYER BRINGS YOUR EXPECTATION INTO REALITY

There is nothing prayer cannot do. Until you pray, you will then realize the reality of God's intentions for you. God does not turn down the expectations of the righteous. The Bible tells us that the expectations of the righteous shall not be cut short. God honors the prayer of His children. Read Genesis 24, Abrahams' servant prayed for God to show him unfailing love by bringing a faithful woman who would marry Isaac, his master's son. He asked God to show him which woman would be fit to marry Isaac. He requested God to bring a woman who would give him water to drink from her jug and provide water to his camel to drink. God answered the servant's requests and turned his expectation into reality.

Elijah boldly declared to Ahab that as surely as the Lord reigns, there will be no rain for three years. The Bible tells us in James 5:17 that Elijah prayed earnestly. We have no power to do anything. All power belongs to God, but He has given us the authority to ask for whatever we want through Christ Jesus, His Son, and we will receive.

God heard the request of Hannah and turned her story from being barren to being fruitful. Peninnah, Hannah's rival, did not expect to see Hannah have a child, but Hannah had an expectation that one day, she would have a child. So, she ran to God and turned her expectation unto God's mighty hands, and He turned her expectation into reality.

Whatever that could be troubling you right now, turn it to God in prayer and be patient, knowing that God whose hands are not tired will bear them all for you. You are not limited to God's glory. He has a place in His heart for you. Just call on Him, and He will answer you and do great and mighty things.

Prayer: *Father of all greatness, I surrender my life to you this day. I cannot do it without you. You are the God of yesterday, today, and forever. Kingdoms will come and go, but you will remain God above all. I lay down myself to you and plead for your mercy. Please forgive me in all areas that I may have gone astray from knowing you as God who reigns in heaven and on earth. Today, I confess that Jesus was sent to die for me, and I declare Jesus as my Lord and personal savior. Father, transform my life for your glory and touch my heart to receive Your Word. Open my ears to hear your Word and help me to act upon them. I am a sinner, and today, I denounce my sins, and by the name of Jesus Christ through the blood that was shed on the cross of Calvary. I break myself loose from every demonic attack. I rebuke every spirit of depression, addiction, mental disorder, anger, sexual behavior, immorality, and condemnation in my life. I drink the cup of life through our Lord Jesus. I pronounce healing and sound mind from today in the name of God the Father, Son, and the Holy Spirit. I confess that I will serve you with all my life. In Jesus' name, I pray. Amen!*

EPILOGUE

Prayer is the simplest thing to do. Yet, we find it hard to do. I want to emphasize that our relationship with God cannot manifest without prayers. God is in heaven, and we cannot walk to heaven by climbing a ladder or boarding an airplane. There is no physical path or contact to meet with God and Jesus, except through prayers and reading the bible.

God's purpose for us is to be His best friends. He has made all things possible for us to keep a good relationship with Him. But as humans, we sometimes negate this path of the relationship because we feel it's a waste of time to maintain a relationship with someone we cannot feel, touch, and see.

God is a Living God, and God with eyes, ears, and hands. Many people wonder how God looks like. They also wonder why they can't see Him. God is the Creator of the universe. The world's existence began with Him, and the end of the world will come from His command. The carnal eyes cannot see God, but the spiritual eyes and a spiritual mind.

When we come to God in prayer, He opens our eyes to see Him, draws us closer to him, and supplies our needs in abundance. We are thankful to God for giving us physical parents whom we can talk to, see, and even sit together to discuss important life issues. But there is always a gap left unfulfilled if we do not have a relationship with our Maker.

Our identity is hidden if we don't realize it. We are born into this world for a purpose, and every purpose and plan in our lives are held in God's hands. Our paths and purposes are hidden from us until God unlocks His plans for us.

ABOUT THE AUTHOR

Roseline Udoetuk is a strong spiritual woman from a small town in Akwa Ibom, Nigeria. She is from a solid spiritual-based background. Her spiritual upbringing helped her to know that prayer is the weapon to fight all battles. One of the best things Roseline has experienced through prayer is peace. Roseline is a minister and a prophetess of God's divine purpose. She is a woman of simple words, a good heart, loving, caring, jovial, and kind. Most importantly, she does not take God out of her plans.

God has used Roseline to touch many lives, including prophesying in God's name, and it comes to pass. He started using her at a very young age to prophesy, and many of God's spoken prophecies have been fulfilled. Though Roseline enjoyed reading Christian books, and her father wrote many spiritual books, she never imagined being a writer.

Someone asked Roseline when she developed the talent for writing, and she responded, *"It's not my talent, but God's will, and maybe God wanted me to continue where my father stopped."* Roseline's father was a spiritual man of God, a writer, a seer, a messenger, a hearer of God's Word, and a faithful servant in God's call and purpose. No wonder they say a fruit does not fall far from its tree. Roseline's writing skill is her father's inheritance.

Death is the call of glory. It saddens Roseline that her father is no longer here to see her spiritual journey and life. Her spiritual growth was what her father was yearning to see in his children. Roseline is a spiritual and inspirational writer who does not write at will but as the

Holy Spirit leads. Roseline's first book is titled "*When God is Involved, Everything Else Doesn't Matter.*"

REFLECTIONS

Reflect on the past five years of your life and ponder on where God is leading you

---

Count your blessings, and you will see they are too many to count

---

If God was not in your life, where would you be?

If men were God, do you think you would live till today?

Name five things that stuck with you after reading this book

List your daily prayer point(s) from each stage of your life

DAILY TO-DO LIST

- Pray before you leave the house
- Watch and listen to Roseline Udoetuk's YouTube Chanel
- Listen to Channel 95:5 (bbn.org)
- Listen to K-Love broadcast
- Listen to Christian or gospel songs
- Take it one day at a time
- Every day comes with its blessings
- Don't live by yesterday
- Let God handle your day
- Smile always, and be encouraged
- No matter the anger, let peace reign
- Tell yourself: I am in God's plan

PURCHASE MY FIRST BOOK, "*WHEN GOD IS INVOLVED, EVERY-THING ELSE DOESN'T MATTER,*" ONLINE.

Thank you for purchasing this book! I pray this book changes your life and May God Bless you abundantly.

PRAYER POINTS

PRAYER POINTS

NOTES